PEACEFUL WORDS

GERMAIN DROOGENBROODT

Translation by the author and Stanley Barkan

ISBN: 978-81-19228-36-2

First Edition: 2023
Rs. 200/-

Cyberwit.net
HIG 45 Kaushambi Kunj, Kalindipuram
Allahabad - 211011 (U.P.) India
http://www.cyberwit.net
Tel: +(91) 9415091004
E-mail: info@cyberwit.net

Printed at Replika.

Contents

THE LIGHT

It dawns,
the sun rises
out of nowhere

ignites
what only apparently
seems to come from afar

although it is near
and within us:

the light.

CINDERS

Although their duration is limited,
the glowing embers spread
what was once fire
warmth and light.

So are also memories
that are not erased—
from better times the cinders,
the enduring glow.

ANCHOR

Not every anchor one throws out
offers safety or discovery
of what is deep and unfathomable.

Anchoring is sometimes a standstill
not farther towards more
than what is visible.

DETACHMENT

But what seeks the bird that flies up
and lifts itself from the earth?

What else does he seeks
than detachment from the things
that are earthly and addictive

—an obstacle

to higher flight.

HEART

Do not listen to the heartbeat
as the ticking of a clock
whose duration is finite.

But as a wonder
that can be heard and felt
in the innermost
of one's own being.

PRECAUTION

Keep from speaking
the silver

from silence
the gold

and of happiness
even the crumbs

that can be provisions
for leaner times.

ELEVATION

The bird that flies up
does not fly
to exalt himself

but to detach itself

—even if only for a moment

from all that is earthly.

BRIDGE

A rainbow is more
than a range of colors
that pleases the eye
but a bridge

—that, just for a moment,

connects heaven and earth.

LAS MONTAÑAS DE BOGOTÁ

We greet you from these sunny but sad mountains of Bogotá.
—Eduardo Bechara Navratilova

Cloudless the sky
bathing in sunlight
the mountains
and among the greenery
resounds the sound
of a variety of birds
the cheerful song,
as if prosperity
would not be for some
but for all,
the sky not too high,
happiness not unattainable
and too far away.

PEACEFUL PANORAMA

Accompanied by birdsong
the dawn appears.

Flowers open
greedily drinking the light
and spreading their perfume.

Over the sharp line of the horizon,
a boat slides over the sea
and the mind
—so turbulent sometimes—
comes for a moment at rest.

WITHOUT WHY

The blossom that opens
and pleases the eye of man
asks no favor in return

selflessly
the blossom gives itself

and dies in beauty
as a flower.

THE UNNAMABLE

Even if one gives a thousand names
to what is unnamable,
the unmentionable
does not reveal its name.

RECOGNITION

Stacked on the writing table the books
multicolored, large and small, thin and thick
poetry from all over the world.

Peaceful words waiting
for the recognition, for the acceptance
of being distinct and different,
to be allowed to be themselves.

INSIGHT

The creation of a poem
is much more than lines
appearing one by one
on the white sheet.

Poetry is also insight
not only shelter
for the word.

BLIND

The blind
can neither experience the budding
of the spring blossoms
nor the splendor of colors
of the autumn trees.
But who can see it
and does not see it
is blinder than the blind
who cannot see.

VANITY

What the wind
says to the trees
and what the leaves whisper
will never decipher a human being
who imagines
to know more
than what he knows.

TO SEE

Closing the eyes
does not always result in reduced vision
but sometimes
—directed inwards—
reveals more
than what is seen.

NET

The freedom
of the fish in the sea
is as long freedom
until he is caught.

So are human beings
only free at their birth
not yet caught
in the net.

HEAVEN

It is not heaven
the bird seeks
when it spreads its wings
and flies up.

It knows,
that also for it
heaven is too far
and inscrutable.

METAMORPHOSIS

The serpent was not driven out
from the earthly paradise.

She stayed there all the time
manifolded
and disguised herself
as human.

THE EARTHLY PARADISE

The earthly paradise
has not been lost.

All those centuries
it has continued to exist
but not for everyone.

ALZHEIMER

Just as the dawn does not suddenly
but gradually arises,
oblivion increases
with the years.

What remains
is the memory of the past
of bygones
which only in memory
know their return.

WORLD PICTURE

It dawns . . .
what was darkness before
dissolves without trace into the light
as if elsewhere darkness
and despair do not reign
as if elsewhere were no people
waiting in vain
for light.

TERROR

The war is no longer declared but continues.
The unheard of has become daily.
—Ingeborg Bachmann

Homes destroyed by missiles,
innocent people, women, children,
killed by the haughty madness
of misleaders.

Unwinged the dove, the truth,
raped by lies.

SOCIAL MEDIA & CO.

Whoever stretches his hand
not only loses his arm
but also his identity.

THE DEFENSELESS WORD

How great is the fear of the word
to leave its shelter
naked and defenseless.

And wherever it appears
again and again
mutilated and raped.

THE DEAD

The dead speak
though one neither hears nor sees them.

They speak with words of silence
which sometimes are more penetrating
than what they ever said before.

INDOCTRINATED INTELLIGENCE

The void
—stripped of all meaning—
has become mundane.

What one should think or do
is preprogrammed.

The image
which we see in the mirror
is no longer our own image.

POLLUTION

Pollution
covers the earth

contaminates oceans and seas
the rivers and the air
kills birds and fish.

How long
will man survive?

VEILED

Sometimes obscured or veiled,
sometimes light in the darkness,
is the moon at night.

She briefly heals the eye
wounded by the excess of images
of injustice and harm
by the despair in the gaze
of a ragged child.

OVERCASTED

There are days
in which darkness
covers and permeates everything.

Happiness that before
used to be generous and abundant
seems unattainable, too far away.

Although one knows
—or hopes—
that never disappears
all the light.

SMART PHONE

In the waiting room
sits a large number of travelers.

With one notable exception
all of them are busy
with a little thing called smart phone
that fascinates them all the time.

With two thumbs at the same time
they write their stories,
meaningful or not they are written,
and sent out into the world.

Only one person does not write, but reads,
he reads a book.
Doesn't he have anything to say?

ILLUMINATION

Not every night
is studded with stars.

And not every day
has a dawn
that with its colors
pleases the eye.

But the artificial light
does not illuminate more
than the near sight.

WITNESSES OF A TIME

Just as the rain
erases traces left behind,
disappears by a technical problem
or decision of higher powers
what we once entrusted
to floppy, computer, VHS or CD.

What will soon remain of us, only yellowed
that once was written on paper
by typewriter or pen—
and of those who come after us,
nothing at all?

ARTIFICIAL INTELLIGENCE

Rivers overflow their banks
houses are demolished
cars swept away
by the raging waters:
man has disrupted nature.

In vain
wisdom's warning words

Would a chip, implanted in the brain,
offer more wisdom or even more blindness
and indoctrination?

USELESS PRAYERS

So many calamities take place on earth
continually and increasingly plagued
by disasters and injustice,
although millions of prayers
are daily sent to heaven.

But which God, who speaks all those languages,
can give them a hearing, when it is man
who disrupts even the heavenly vault?

DIGNIFIED

For a bird
that cannot fly anymore
life is no more life.

But is life
that is no longer dignified
still life?

SIGN

What else is the lightning
which illuminates the sky for just a moment
than a sign to man
that everything earthly
is ephemeral and transient?

EPHEMERE

Although the day flower
lives no more than a day, she doesn't mourn,
but she gives her beauty

—even if it lasts but one day,

her whole life.

NON-RECURRING

Life is like a book
that word for word
but never again
is read
and from which no human
but life itself
turns the pages.

AUTUMN

The leaves die off,
but they do not grieve.

Multicolored adorned
they leave their tree
in a last dance.

MIGRATION

The migration of birds
leads to the warmer,
to their familiar regions.

A long
or short migratory journey
is like human life.

But neither the day
nor the destiny is known.

MORE

Withered leaves
are more than died-off green
but fertility
for the earth.

So are also deceased more
than died-off life
entrusted to the earth.

WHAT REMAINS

The water wheel
doesn’t count
the drops of the stream.

Just as life neither counts
the hours of a human’s life.

Only the time clock
counts down the days,
the remaining time.

IMPOTENCE

Morning after morning
he goes to the beach

With the songs of the birds
and the blooms of the flowers
he shares the joy, the meaning of life.

But in the insistence of the waves
he experiences futility,
the fruitless resistance,
against the passage of time.

THE UNFATHOMABLE

The unfathomable
is not only what exits
beyond recognition.

Unfathomable
is also one's own being
and the soul,

and whether it exists
or whatever it is.

SOUL

What is invisible
to the eye may exist

but not of everything
that is invisible
is one also sure
that it exists.

INTENSITY

It is not the length of time
that makes love
or suffering
greater

but the intensity

the height
or the depth
that remained.

SHADOWS

Of some days
the shadows are so long
that the light seems too far
or not present.

Although one knows
that there is no shadow
without light.

THE COMING AND THE GOING

In the insistence of the waves
crashing against the cliffs
and in the appearence
and disappearance
of the wind he experiences
the limitation of life —
the coming and the going.

REVERSIBLE

"The irreversible
is the step we have not taken"
—Hugo Mujica

Pushing the boundaries
beyond the perceptibility.

Turning the irreversible into reversible
when the road to farther
no more offers a farther.

ULTIMATE EQUALITY

How high ever the flight
for rich and poor alike,
life is a path
taking everyone
in the same direction —
to the same end.

WHERE TO?

In the hospital
listens the dying
to the beating
of his own heart
beating irregularly
slower and slower.

He knows the road
wonders
where to?

BORROWED DAWN

With its hand of shadow and darkness ,
the defenseless light
unravels the evening

unravels the future
the magic
the borrowed dawn

pulls out the wick
sheds the oil
extinguishes time.

LONELY GOODBYE

for those who, wherever, have to die lonely

Chilly the room
the white walls.

Audible only
the echo of loneliness.

Not a tender word anymore,
no warm embrace.

Just the time,
a leaking tap,
ticking.

None knocking at the door
nobody you expect,
no one, except death.

WAR IN UKRAINE

The almond trees are here in bloom
a delight to the eye
that loves beauty.

Soon the citrus blossoms
will spread their seductive perfume.

But elsewhere rages the war,
the destruction and human suffering.

No blossoms bloom there—
they suffocate in the smoke
of barbarous violence.

PEACE DOVE

It is raining
it is rains sadness.

For innocent victims
for the destruction of a country
for the escape of murderous violence.

Hungry, a turtle dove leaves
from the shelter of her tree.

Like a noose
the black ring around her neck.

DESPOT

The night has assaulted the dawn
and steals from peace
the precious light.

Silence dies down
drowned out by gunfire
cannons and howling sirens.

Unmoved by the suffering
—even of his own people—
the power-mad despot.

HOPE

It is winter,
the chilly wind has torn off
the last leaves from the trees
which before were protection
and accommodation for the birds.

They shiver in the cold
but still whistle
because they also hope
for better times.

Germain Droogenbroodt, was born 11 September 1944 in Rollegem, the Flemish part of Belgium. In 1987 he moved to the Mediterranean artist village of Altea and integrated in Spanish literary life.

Germain Droogenbroodt is an internationally appreciated poet, invited yearly at the most prestigious international poetry festivals. He wrote short stories and literary reviews, but mainly poetry, so far sixteen poetry books, published in 30 countries. He is also translator, publisher, and promoter of modern international poetry. He translated – he speaks six languages – more than thirty collections of German, Italian, Spanish, Latin American, English and French poetry, including anthologies of Bertolt Brecht, Mahmud Darwish, Reiner Kunze, Miguel Hernández, José Ángel Valente, Francisco Brines and also rendered Arabic, Chinese, Japanese, Persian and Korean poetry into Dutch.

As founder and editor of the Belgian publishing house POINT Editions (**PO**etry **INT**ernational) he published more than eighty collections of mainly modern, international poetry. In 1996 he set up a new poetic movement, called *neo-sensacionismo* with the famous Chinese poets Bei Dao and Duo Duo

Germain Droogenbroodt organised and co-organised several international poetry festivals in Spain. He is vice president of the Academy Mihai Eminescu, organizing the International Poetry Festival Mihai Eminescu in Craiova, Romania, co-founder, and advisor of JUNPA (Japan Universal Poets Association), artistic advisor of the Italian movement Poetry & Discovery, general counsel of the Chinese cultural Association Huifeng, International Shanghai and is founding president of the Spanish cultural foundation ITHACA. He also collaborates with the Italian poetry publication Margutte.

His poetic oeuvre is many-sided. After his début with "Forty at the wall" (1984), defined as neo-romantic poetry, he published "Do you know the country?", *Meditations at Lake* Como (Italy), a collection of nature poems. In 1995 he was awarded a Hawthornden Fellowship (Scotland) where he wrote "CONVERSATION WITH THE HEREAFTER", poems about death, awarded in Belgium with the P.G. Buckinx-Prize and "PALPABLE ABSENCE", a bilingual (Dutch Spanish) collection of love poems. A critic of the Dutch Information Office for Libraries described his love poems as "virtuoso poetry". At the end of 1998 appeared "BETWEEN THE SILENCE OF YOUR LIPS", his collected love poems.

During his sojourn at the Palace-Fortress "Neemrana" in Rajasthan, 1998, he completed the poetry cycle "THE ROAD", (read TAO) a poetic bridge between the East and the West, inspiring the Flemish artist Frans Minnaert and the Indian painter Satish Gupta, who enriched "The Road" with their drawings. This philosophical, mystical poetry is so far his most popular book, published already in 25 countries, according to the Icelandic poet-critic Thór Stefansson prophetic, philosophic poetry, translated by such famous poets as Bei Dao (Chinese), Fuad Rifka (Arabic), Jana Stroblova and Josef Hruby (Czech), Milan Richter (Slovak), Emilio Coco, Luca Benassi and Tiziana Orrù (Italian), Ganga Prasad Vimal (Hindi)...In 2001 he wrote in Spanish "AMANECE EL CANTOR" (The Singer Awakes), a homage to the deceased poet José Ángel Valente, followed by "COUNTERLIGHT" written in Ronda (Southern Spain) in 2002, published in Spain by Calima Ediciones, in Romania by ex Ponto, in Belgium by POINT Editions, in both Mongolian languages by GCompress Co., Ltd. Ulaanbaatar, in Arab by Albayat (Morocco), in Hong Kong by "Contemporary Poetry", and in Taiwan by Poet Culture. Corp. The latter publication includes also "COUNTERLIGHT."

His poetry book "IN THE STREAM OF TIME, *Meditations in the Himalayas*", was published in 2008 in Belgium and as part of "Selected Poems by Germain Droogenbroodt", 2008 in Shanghai by the Shanghai Literature & Art Publishing Group and in Spain, laureate of the *XXIX Premio de Poesía Juan Alcaide 2008.* **Struga Poetry Evenings** also published "IN THE STREAM OF TIME" in their prestigious "Pleiades" in

2010. The book was also translated in Japanese and launched at the Kyoto City International Foundation in Kyoto, Japan in 2010 and in Gaelic (Irish) in 2012. A selection of his poems was also published in Bengal in Bangladesh (2012 and 2015). "UNSHADOWED LIGHT", was launched end 2012 in a bilingual Dutch-Spanish publication at the Book Fair in Antwerp and in several Belgian towns and in Spain. "IN THE STREAM OF TIME, *Meditations in the Himalayas*" was published in Romania in 2015.

The anthology "THE DEWDROPS OF DAWN," a selection from 11 poetry books, was published with illustrations by Satish Gupta in German, in Dutch and in Croatian (2014). "DEWDROPS", a selection of 100 haiku in Japanese, English, Spanish, and Dutch was published by JUNPA, Kyoto, and launched in Japan end 2016. His last but one poetry book, "THE EPHEMERAL FLOWER OF TIME" was published end 2016 in Dutch and Spanish and in English (2017) and in 2021 in Serbia, in Japan and in China. "THE ORACLE OF TIME", published 2019 in the US. His last but one book "The Unrest of the Word" was published Dutch-Spanish in Belgium and Holland and Dancing Butterfly, his second collection of haiku, as published end 2022 in Japan. THE ROAD OF BEING, his latest poetry book, will be published begin 2023 in Belgium, Holland, Chile, Albania and in Italy.

Several famous artists made paintings and sculptures inspired by his poetry as international composers composed music to poems, such as the Dutch composer Bart Bakker who composed the "*Germain Droogenbroodt cycle,*" 12 pieces for flute.

Germain Droogenbroodt is yearly invited to give recitals and conferences at universities and at the most prestigious poetry festivals around the world. He was recommended for the Nobel prize of Literature 2017.

www.ingramcontent.com/pod-product-compliance
Lightning Source LLC
LaVergne TN
LVHW040955150826
845672LV00002B/712

9788119228362